# *The* ROAD TO
# HAPPINESS

*≈ Simple Secrets to a Happy Life ≈*

MAC ANDERSON AND BJ GALLAGHER

Cover and internal design by: Vieceli Design Company, West Dundee, Illinois

Photo Credits: Images courtesy iStockphoto.com and Thinkstock.

Published by Simple Truths, an imprint of Sourcebooks, Inc.
P.O. Box 4410, Naperville, Illinois 60567-4410
(630) 961-3900
Fax: (630) 961-2168
www.sourcebooks.com

Printed and bound in China.
FCP 10 9 8 7 6 5 4 3 2

# TABLE OF CONTENTS

It's good to be **JUST PLAIN HAPPY.**
It's a little better to know that
*you're happy*; but *to understand*
that you're happy and *to know*
*why* and how and still be happy—
**BE HAPPY IN THE BEING AND**
**THE KNOWING**—well, that is
beyond happiness, *that is bliss.*

≈ *Henry Miller, writer* ≈

# INTRODUCTION

When I travel on business, I like to talk to the taxi drivers who take me from the airport to my hotel, or to a convention center, or to a restaurant. Taxi drivers are often immigrants with interesting personal histories and unusual cultural backgrounds. I ask them how long they've been in America, how they chose which city to live in, and what they like best about where they live. Of course, I also ask them for advice on good local restaurants and any special attractions they'd recommend to a visitor. I've had some great experiences on my travels, thanks to the advice of taxi drivers!

On one trip about ten years ago, I was making conversation with the taxi driver, asking him my usual questions about how he came to live where he lived. Then I asked him a hypothetical question: *"If you could live anywhere in the world—and if money was no object—where would you live?"*

Without hesitating for even a second, he replied, "I live in my heart. So it really doesn't matter where my body lives. If I am happy inside, then I live in Paradise, no matter where my residence is."

I felt humbled and a little foolish for my question. Of course he was right—happiness is an inside job. He had reminded me of something I already knew,

but had forgotten. ***If you can't find happiness inside yourself, you'll never find it in the outside world, no matter where you move. Wherever you go, there you are. You take yourself with you.***

I am grateful for the wisdom of that taxi driver. And I'm grateful for all the wisdom others have shared with me about how to be happy.

I asked my good friend BJ Gallagher to join me in gathering some of our favorite bits of wisdom and advice to share with you in this slender volume. We hope the stories, poems, anecdotes, and quotes will enrich your life as much as they have ours.

**MAC ANDERSON**
*Founder, Simple Truths*

# HAPPINESS IS ...

## An attitude of gratitude.

BE THANKFUL FOR WHAT YOU HAVE;
YOU'LL END UP HAVING MORE. IF YOU CONCENTRATE
ON WHAT YOU DON'T HAVE, YOU WILL NEVER,
EVER HAVE ENOUGH.

*≈ Oprah Winfrey, media entrepreneur ≈*

# THANKFUL

*by* NANCIE J. CARMODY

❀

*A thankful spirit is a healthy spirit.* As the twists and turns of life lead to feelings of being out of control, sometimes our attitude is all that we have control over. … the following reflection may help you develop a thankful attitude. Sometimes life is all about how we look at it!

**I am thankful for . . .**

❀ *the mess to clean after a party because it means I have been surrounded by friends.*

❀ *the taxes I pay because it means that I am employed.*

❀ *a lawn that needs mowing, windows that need cleaning and gutters that need fixing because it means I have a home.*

❀ *my shadow who watches me work because it means I am out in the sunshine.*

❀ *the spot I find at the far end of the parking lot because it means I am capable of walking.*

❊ all the complaining I hear about our government because it means we have freedom of speech.

❊ my huge heating bill because it means I am warm.

❊ the lady behind me in church who sings off key because it means that I can hear.

❊ the alarm that goes off early in the morning hours because it means that I am alive.

❊ the piles of laundry and ironing because it means my loved ones are nearby.

❊ weariness and aching muscles at the end of the day because it means I have been productive.

*(This reflection first appeared in the newsletter of First Presbyterian Church in Lyons, New York. It was reprinted in Family Circle magazine in 1999.)*

> *We tend to forget that happiness doesn't come as a result of getting something we don't have, but rather of recognizing and appreciating what we do have.*
>
> *Frederick Koenig, German inventor*

# GRATITUDE

unlocks the fullness of life. It turns what we have into enough, and more. It turns denial into acceptance, chaos to order, confusion to clarity. It can turn a meal into a feast, a house into a home, a stranger into a friend. Gratitude makes sense of our past, brings peace for today, and creates a vision for tomorrow.

≈ *Melody Beattie, therapist, author* ≈

# ❄ WEATHER REPORT

*by BJ Gallagher*

"Any day I'm vertical
is a good day"…
that's what I always say.
And I give thanks for my health.

## If you ask me,
## "How are you?"
## I'll answer, "GREAT!"
because in saying so,
I make it so.
And I give thanks I can choose my attitude.

When Life gives me dark clouds and rain,
I appreciate the moisture
which brings a soft curl to my hair.

When Life gives me sunshine,
I gratefully turn my face up
to feel its warmth on my cheeks.

When Life brings fog,
  I hug my sweater around me
    and give thanks for the cool shroud of mystery
      that makes the familiar seem different and intriguing.

  When Life brings snow,
I dash outside to catch the first flakes on my tongue,
    relishing the icy miracle that is a snowflake.

# Life's events and experiences are like the weather —
## they come and go,
no matter what my preference.

  So, what the heck?!
I might as well decide to enjoy them.

  For indeed,
    there IS a time for every purpose
      under Heaven.

  Each season brings its own unique blessings.
    And I give thanks.

When we choose
*not* to focus on what is
missing from our lives
but are grateful for
the abundance that's
present...we experience
heaven on earth.

≈ *Sarah Ban Breathnach, author* ≈

## HAPPINESS IS ...

# *Enjoying simple pleasures.*

ALL THAT IS REQUIRED TO FEEL THAT HERE AND
NOW IS HAPPINESS, IS A SIMPLE, FRUGAL HEART.

*≈ Nikos Kazantzakis, Greek novelist ≈*

# SAVOR *the* MOMENT

*by* MAC ANDERSON

*I once heard someone say, "We don't remember days; we remember moments." However, at today's hectic pace we often forget to savor small pleasures while we make big plans.*

In the race to be better or best, we sometimes lose sight of just being. And just being, just soaking in and savoring a beautiful moment, can provide some of life's greatest pleasures. A crackling fire on a cold winter night, a good book, a love letter from your sweetheart, a spectacular sunset, a great meal, or a timeless moment with your child or a good friend ... these moments, if we stop long enough to enjoy, are the essence of a happy and fulfilled life.

I love to fish, especially for large-mouth bass. About three years ago, I was watching television late one night and got this crazy notion to go fishing in the lake behind my house. Of course, my wife thought I was nuts. It was almost midnight!

I convinced her I was sane and took off. I walked out to a warm summer breeze and looked up at the starry sky and breathtaking full moon.

*I allowed my senses to soak in every second—the sweet smell of honeysuckle, the sound of every cricket, the moon's reflection dancing off the water—it was a perfect night.*

After walking across a small field, I took out a flashlight and selected a lure.

On my first cast, I reeled in a bass weighing over five pounds, one of the largest I had ever caught. I gently released it back into the water and continued my midnight adventure. During the next two hours, I caught seventeen bass, all between two and five pounds. Although I've fished for almost fifty years, no fishing memory can top that warm summer night.

But that night provided far more than a fishing memory. It was a life memory. It provided me a snapshot of what life could be like if I just slowed down enough to savor the moments. On my way back to the house, as I walked through the tall grass, I took one last look at the sky and stopped to say

*"Thank you, God, for giving me this night."*

# Enjoy the little things,
for one day you may look back and
realize they were the big things.

*≈ Robert Brault ≈*

# 30

# SATISFYING SIMPLE PLEASURES

*by* MARC HACK

*Life is filled with simple pleasures, the little satisfying (things)
you (don't) anticipate, but always take great pleasure in:*

1   Sleeping In on a Rainy Day

2   Finding Money You Didn't Know You Had

3   Making Brief Eye Contact with Someone
You're Attracted To

4   Skinny Dipping

5   Receiving a Real Letter or Package via Snail Mail

*(continued)*

21  Reminiscing About Old Times with Your Closest Friends

22  Receiving an Unexpected Compliment

23  Having a Good Laugh

24  Feeling Tired, But Good, After a Healthy Workout

25  The Celebration in the Instant Something Makes Sense

26  Relaxing Outdoors on a Sunny Day

27  Holding Hands with Someone You Love

28  Playing in the Water

29  Making Someone Smile or Laugh

30  Finishing What You Started

A comprehensive list of life's simple pleasures would be quite extensive. My list represents those which are most satisfying to a sample of people in and around my life. With a few … exceptions, I believe these simple pleasures hold universal appeal.

*~ Source: marcandangel.com*

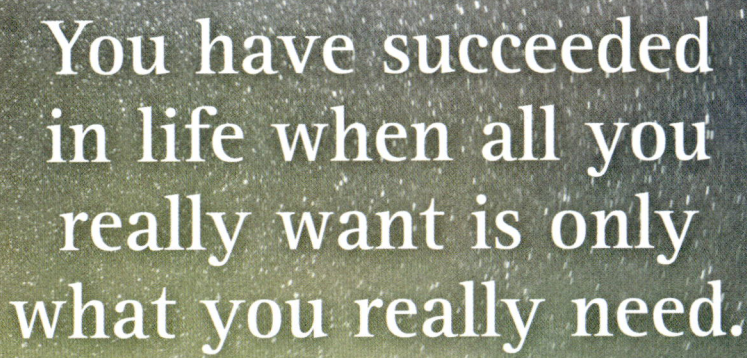

You have succeeded
in life when all you
really want is only
what you really need.

*≈ Vernon Howard, spiritual teacher, author ≈*

❊

# HAPPINESS IS ...

## An Inside Job

SUCCESS IS NOT THE KEY TO HAPPINESS.
HAPPINESS IS THE KEY TO SUCCESS.
IF YOU LOVE WHAT YOU ARE DOING,
YOU WILL BE SUCCESSFUL.

*≈ Herman Cain, businessman, author, speaker ≈*

# HAPPINESS *is an* INSIDE JOB

*by* CHELLIE CAMPBELL

*Studies have shown that, once above subsistence level, having more money and material success won't make you any happier.* You already have to be happy. If you haven't learned how to be a happy person, how to take pleasure in the daily gifts the world offers to all of us, material goods will not satisfy you. Everyone can point to rich people who are lonely, bored,

angry or depressed. Having money just made them comfortable in their misery. The single-minded pursuit of money can distract them from their despair for awhile, but in the end, if they are curled up in their castle alone with no friends, all their millions will be cold comfort.

*Some people are afraid to have a lot of money, because they think the money will make them selfish, uncaring, lonely and miserable.* But money doesn't do that. It's what is done with the money that is either good or evil. If you would do evil if you had money, then you are evil now—just without power. Money does provide power. The more money you have, the more you can manifest your material desires. The downside is that one can get distracted by all the material manifestations and neglect the spiritual ones. But of course, being poor can keep you focused on the lack of material success, and that can keep you from manifesting your spiritual desires.

## So what is the answer?
# Learn to live rich, inside and out.

There is joy in both internal wealth and external wealth. Focus on joy, happiness, your relationship with God, your relationships with other people, the meaning of life, and the mission of your life. Rich or poor, you can meditate and pray and make these your priorities. When you are joyful and grateful for what you have, you create the space for more. When you sense that there is a purpose to life and a mission within it for you to fulfill, then you act in harmony with God and the Universe. Open yourself to manifesting abundance in all areas of life, including financial success, knowing that you will use them honorably and with wisdom for the good of all around you.

*~ Source: The Wealthy Spirit by Chellie Campbell*

*We don't see things as they are ...*
*We see things as we are.*

*≈ Anaïs Nin, French-born diarist ≈*

Ever since happiness heard your name, it has been running through the streets trying to find you.

*Hafiz, Persian Sufi poet*

Happiness *is*

# WISDOM...

**W** ondrous

**I** nsight

**S** eeing

**D** eeply

**O** ffering

**M** iracles

## HAPPINESS IS ...

# *Knowing that the best things in life aren't things.*

BE HAPPY.
IT'S ONE WAY OF BEING WISE.

≈ *Sidonie Gabrielle, French novelist* ≈

# VALUES

*by* MAC ANDERSON

❄

*Earl Nightingale said: "Everything that's really worthwhile in life comes to us free—our minds, our souls, our bodies, our hopes, our dreams, our intelligence, our love of family and friends and country. All of these priceless possessions are free."*

Think about it. You can lose all of your money and start over. If your house burns down, you can rebuild it. It's the things that cost you nothing that you can never replace.

One of the most important keys to living a happy life is to clearly identify your core values. You must decide what matters most. Why the need to identify  your values? Many people think, "I know what's important, I don't need a list to remind me." What they don't fully understand, however, is that core values often serve as critical guides for making important decisions. When you're in doubt, your values will cut through the fog like a beacon in the night.

We all know there are many distractions along the road of life that will try to pull us away from our values. Sometimes we are forced to make difficult choices. But a good rule of thumb is that when you have to sacrifice material possessions for one of those free things that life has given you ... you've made the right choice for a happy and fulfilled life.

That is the *key* to happiness.

## HAPPINESS IS ...

# *Time spent with loved ones.*

THERE IS ONLY ONE HAPPINESS IN THIS LIFE,
TO LOVE AND BE LOVED.

*≈ George Sand, French Romantic writer ≈*

# HAPPINESS *is* GRANDKIDS

*by* ERIC HARVEY

Little did I know how much my happiness would skyrocket when I became a grandfather—the increase was exponential! Don't get me wrong —I enjoyed being a parent, too, and I cherish my two daughters. *But being a grandpa is a whole different thing—transforming my life in ways I never would have predicted.*

I have always thought of myself as a basically happy guy. I am a successful entrepreneur who loves his work. For many years, I worked hard to build my business, traveling frequently, putting in long hours, and reaping the fruits of my labors. I made time for my girls, of course—going to school plays, sporting events, and parent-teacher conferences. We enjoyed family birthdays, holidays, and occasional vacations. My daughters grew up to be beautiful, talented, well-adjusted young women.

As I got older, several serious health crises forced me to cut back on business travel, work shorter hours, and take time to recover. Then my first grandchild was born and I began to re-evaluate my priorities, my time commitments, and my lifestyle. I was suddenly less concerned with hustling for financial success and more concerned with the people in my life. Time, too, became more plentiful as I learned how to manage it better.  *(continued)*

*True happiness is of a retired nature,*
*and an enemy to pomp and noise; it arises,*
*in the first place, from the enjoyment of one's self;*
*and in the next, from the friendship and*
*conversation of a few select companions.*

*≈ Joseph Addison, English dramatist ≈*

My wife and I were presented with five grandkids within four years—a bounty of blessings, for sure! Three of them live here in Dallas and the other two are in North Carolina. My wife and I bought a second home in North Carolina so we could spend plenty of time with both sets of kids. We probably spend one-third of the year in North Carolina and the other two-thirds here in Texas.

**One of the things I committed to doing was spending one-on-one time with each grandchild, creating memorable moments and experiences.** I didn't want to just let things happen by happenstance—I wanted to make things happen. For instance, on each child's birthday, my wife and I take the birthday kid on a two- or three-day trip. So that's five short trips every year, planned around the interests of each child.

> One word *frees us* of all the weight and pain of life – that word is
>
> # LOVE.
>
> *Sophocles,*
> *ancient Greek playwright*

**I like to do activities with the kids that enrich their learning, broadening their appreciation of the world around them, stimulating their curiosity.** We go to science places and museums. We eat at foreign restaurants, where I encourage the kids to try new flavors. For instance, recently we took the four-year-old out for sushi and when I asked her what she wanted to eat there, she replied, "Snake tails." The restaurant didn't have snake tails, but they did have eel, and that's what she ate. How many four-year-olds do you know who would be adventurous enough to eat eel?

It's not that we don't do "normal" things – because we do. Every once in awhile we'll go to McDonalds, and we've been to theme parks and zoos, of course. But in general, we emphasize out-of-the-ordinary places to go, see and do.

And I'm always open to spontaneous adventures with the kids. I carry a kite in the trunk of each of my two cars, so that if we're out with one or more of the grandkids and the wind is just right, we simply stop the car and fly a kite. Now, that's happiness! *(continued)*

35

We let the kids make their own homemade pizzas when they come for a sleepover. "You eat what you make" is the motto for the evening … and they've created some pretty wild pizza toppings from time to time.

Every year, we take two family vacations—one in summer and one over the Christmas holidays—we take both our kids, their spouses, and all five grandkids for a family getaway.

We've given each of the kids their own piggybanks and taught them about saving money. When Mother's Day rolls around, we help the kids go shopping for their moms—they pay for half the gift they pick out and I pay for the other half.

About six years ago, I started organizing family photos from all our trips and activities and editing them into a 40-minute DVD, "Family Year in Review." I include music, narration and titles to make it as polished and professional as I can. At Christmas, I give everyone in the family a copy of the DVD. It's my way of creating a legacy.

I could go on and on with all the things I've been doing to enjoy my grandkids, but you get the idea. I think the secret to have a great experience as a grandparent is: *"Manage the behaviors that control the outcomes."* Don't wait for cool things to happen—take the initiative to make them happen.

*Happiness isn't where you find it …*
*happiness is where you create it.*

# CELEBRATE

the happiness that friends are always giving;
Make every day a holiday and celebrate just living!

≈ *Amanda Bradley* ≈

❋

Happiness *is*

# TRUE FRIENDS...

**T** rust

**R** espect

**U** nderstanding

**E** mpathy

**F** orgiveness

**R** esponsiveness

**I** nsight

**E** xpressions of love

**N** eeding one another

**D** ependability

**S** piritual connection

Life is partly *what we make it*, and partly what is made by the FRIENDS WE CHOOSE.

≈ *Tennessee Williams, playwright* ≈

## HAPPINESS IS ...

# *Serving others and contributing to the world.*

WHAT WE HAVE DONE FOR OURSELVES ALONE
DIES WITH US; WHAT WE HAVE DONE FOR OTHERS AND
THE WORLD REMAINS AND IS IMMORTAL.

*≈ Albert Pike, soldier, writer, Freemason ≈*

# THE GOLDEN RULE

## *by* MAC ANDERSON

❄

I grew up in Trenton, a west Tennessee town of five thousand people. I have wonderful memories of those first eighteen years, and many people in Trenton influenced my life in very positive ways. My football coach, Walter Kilzer, taught me the importance of hard work, discipline, and believing in myself. My history teacher, Fred Culp, is still the funniest person I've ever met. *He taught me that a sense of humor, and especially laughing at yourself, can be one of life's greatest blessings.*

But my father was my hero. He taught me many things, but at the top of the list, he taught me to treat people with love and respect ... to live the Golden Rule. I remember one particular instance of him teaching this "life lesson" as if it were yesterday. Dad owned a furniture store, and I used to dust the furniture every Wednesday after school to earn my allowance. One afternoon I observed my Dad talking to all the customers as they came in—the hardware store owner, the banker, a farmer, a doctor. At the end of the day, just as Dad was closing, the garbage collector came in.

I was ready to go home, and I thought that surely Dad wouldn't spend too much time with him. But I was wrong. Dad greeted him at the door with a big hug and talked with him about his wife and son who had been in a car accident the month before. He empathized, he asked questions, he listened, and he listened some more. I kept looking at the clock, and when the man finally left, I asked, "Dad, why did you spend so much time with him? He's just the garbage collector." Dad then looked at me, locked the front door to the store, and said, "Son, let's talk."

*He said, "I'm your father and I tell you lots of stuff as all fathers should, but if you remember nothing else I ever tell you, remember this ... treat every human being just the way that you would want to be treated."* He said, "I know this is not the first time you've heard it, but I want to make sure it's the first time you truly understand it, because if you had understood, you would never have said what you said." We sat there and talked for another hour about the meaning and the power of the Golden Rule. Dad said, *"If you live the Golden Rule everything else in life will usually work itself out, but if you don't, your life probably will be very unhappy and without meaning."*

The Golden Rule, "treat others the way you wish to be treated" is much more than a statement. It's an attitude that exudes kindness, compassion and respect for others. And I can say with conviction that I've never met a person who lived the Golden Rule that wasn't happy. Poet Marianne Moore said it best: *"The heart that gives, gathers."*

I've learned that people will *forget* what you said;
People will *forget* what you did;
But people will *never forget*

# HOW YOU MADE THEM FEEL.

*≈ Maya Angelou, poet, professor, actress ≈*

## Recipe for happiness

**2 heaping cups of patience**
**1 heart full of love**
**2 hands full of generosity**

**1 head full of understanding**
**A dash of laughter**

*Sprinkle generously with kindness. Add plenty of faith and mix well.*
*Spread over a period of a lifetime and serve everyone you meet.*

*~ Author unknown*

**HAPPINESS** *is not* an individual matter. When you are able to bring relief, or bring back the smile to one person, not only that person **PROFITS**, *but you also profit*. The deepest happiness you can have comes from that capacity to help relieve the **SUFFERING** of others. So if we have the **HABIT** of being peace, then *there is a natural tendency* for us to go in the direction of service. Nothing compels us, except the joy of **SHARING** peace, the joy of sharing **FREEDOM** from *afflictions*, freedom from worries, freedom from craving, which are the *true foundations* for happiness.

≈ *Thich Nhat Hanh, Vietnamese Buddhist teacher & author* ≈

❋

## HAPPINESS IS ...

# *Surrounding yourself with positive, happy people.*

SOME CAUSE HAPPINESS WHEREVER THEY GO;
OTHERS, WHENEVER THEY GO.

*≈ Oscar Wilde, Irish poet, novelist, dramatist ≈*

# HAPPINESS
## *is* CONTAGIOUS

❄

*Not too long ago, researchers from the Harvard Medical School and the University of California at San Diego made an important discovery—happiness is contagious.* Your happiness is influenced not only by the people you know, but also by the people they know. In other words, happiness spreads through social relationships—groups, cliques, teams, clubs, clans, communities, gangs, neighborhoods and families.

Sadness is contagious, too, but it seems to spread much less efficiently, according to one of the coauthors of the study, Dr. James Fowler, of U.C. San Diego.

Fowler explains how your happiness is affected by people you don't even know: *"We have known for a long time that there is a direct relationship between one person's happiness and another's. But this study shows that indirect relationships also affect happiness. We found a statistical relationship not just between your happiness and your friends' happiness, but between your happiness and your friends' friends' friends' happiness."*

Fowler and his colleague, Nicholas Christakis of Harvard, discovered that there are three degrees of separation when it comes to happiness:

**15%** *If your friend, family member, or other direct social contact is happy, your probability of happiness increases by 15%.*

**10%** *If the spouse of your friend, or the boss of your spouse, or some other second-degree social contact is happy, your probability of happiness increases by 10%.*

**6%** *And if the friend of a friend of your best friend, or some other third-degree social contact is happy, your probability of happiness increases by 6%.*

Having more friends will also increase your chance of happiness, but not as much as having happy friends. With regard to happiness, quality seems to be more important than quantity.

*Want more happiness in your life?*
*Hang around happy people.*

Friendship *improves* happiness and abates misery
by doubling our joys and dividing our grief.

≈ *Marcus Tullius Cicero, poet and philosopher* ≈

> All who would win joy must share it;
> Happiness was born a twin.
>
> *Lord Byron, English poet*

Happiness *lives in*

# COMMUNITY...

- **C** oming together
- **O** pen arms, open hearts, open minds
- **M** utual respect
- **M** utual support
- **U** nderstanding differences
- **N** ever losing sight of common goals
- **I** ntegrity—both individual and collective
- **T** rust and truth
- **Y** ielding to one another in healthy interdependence

HAPPINESS IS ...

# *Finding humor in everyday situations.*

ANGELS CAN FLY BECAUSE THEY TAKE
THEMSELVES LIGHTLY.

*≈ G.K. Chesterton, British author ≈*

# RECIPE *for* DISASTER

*by* KATHLEEN EVERETT

❋

*For generations, women have supported each other through difficult times.* Some rush to the side of the friend in crisis, giving generously of their time and good advice. Others drag the miserable one out for a much-needed night of dancing and play. When I hear a friend's bad news, I head straight into the kitchen to tie one on—an apron, that is—hoping I'll be able to say with butter, flour and sugar what I can't put into words.

"Suzanne, I am so sorry to hear about your mother. Here is a loaf of cinnamon bread. I kneaded it in my little kitchen where the windows face east so the sun and the bread could rise together this morning. She seemed like a really nice woman. I'd love to hear more stories about her when you're ready to tell them. I hope you like raisins."

"Aimee, I am shocked that he left you for the dental hygienist. I don't have the name of a lawyer to give you, but I did bring you a casserole. I'm naming it, 'You're Too Good for That Jerk Chicken.' It goes really well with cheap merlot. You won't feel bad forever. I promise. Call me before you do anything drastic."

"Cheryl, no one will think that guinea pig died of neglect. It was nice of you to volunteer to take care of it over the break. I'm sure the teacher will understand. It was probably about 108 in human years. Here are two dozen 'Cheer Up Chocolate Chip Cookies' for strength while you deliver the bad news. Try to save a few for the kids."

"Edith, I know the chemo might affect your appetite, so I filled your freezer with containers. Six of them are 'You're No Chicken Soup' with plenty of nettle, prayers and garlic in it. The others are ravioli I shaped into hearts for when you need a reminder of how dearly loved you are, and it comes with unlimited refills. You will be well again."

When Angela across the street called to say that her brother had a stroke, I headed once again to the kitchen, this time to make a basket of food and a thermos of coffee for the long ride ahead of her. I expected she would drive straight through the 700 miles and not stop for meals. And knowing Angela, she'd be crying all the way across Ohio, so I put extra salt in the egg salad to make up for all those tears.

While I packed, the cell phone in my apron pocket delivered a text message from my daughter: "Samantha's boyfriend broke up with her. Do you think I should make lavender cupcakes or a nutmeg torte?"

A new generation, another woman, amassing her own collection of recipes for disaster.

*The person who knows how to laugh at himself
will never cease to be amused.*

≈ *Shirley MacLaine, actress, dancer*≈

The gift of

# LAUGHTER...

**L** oving life, with its ups and downs

**A** ppreciating what's right with the world

**U** nderstanding your own quirks and eccentricities

**G** oing for the gusto (and the guffaw!)

**H** aving fun wherever and whenever you can

**T** aking life seriously, but taking yourself lightly

**E** ager to embrace life's lunacies

**R** eady to grin at every opportunity

## HAPPINESS IS ...

# *Setting yourself up for success.*

**IF YOU WANT TO LIVE A HAPPY LIFE, TIE IT TO A GOAL, NOT TO PEOPLE OR THINGS.**

*≈ Albert Einstein, German-born Nobel Laureate in Physics≈*

# CATCH YOURSELF *doing something right ... or*
# APPROXIMATELY RIGHT

### *by* BJ GALLAGHER

❉

My friend Kathryn has only one rule in her life: "I'm not allowed to beat myself up." She elaborates: "I got more than enough criticism and abuse when I was growing up. There were plenty of people beating me up, verbally and emotionally, if not physically. *So now my only rule is—no matter what I do—I am not allowed to beat myself up."*

Kathryn told me how, years ago, she decided to go to the gym and start working out. She was overweight and self-conscious, but determined to do something about it. She got in her car and drove to the gym, where she parked in the parking structure. Kathryn walked from her car to the large picture window on the front of the gym, where she peered in at the svelte girls in their leggings, workout clothes, and yoga pants—then she turned around and went home. She just couldn't bring herself to go in. But instead of berating herself, she patted herself on the back. "Good girl," Kathryn said to herself, "You went to the gym." She had honored her commitment to herself—at least she got to the front window.

Maybe next time she would manage to walk in the door. Perhaps she could work her way up to getting a locker. After that, maybe she could muster the courage to take a yoga class. And each step of the way, no matter how tiny that step was, Kathryn would tell herself, "Good girl, you showed up. You did what you said you would do for yourself."

> Inch by inch,
> ## IT'S A CINCH;
> Yard by yard,
> it's really hard.
>
> *Mom*

I can't tell you how many times Kathryn's story has helped me. A tiny step toward a goal is still a step. I don't have to make giant leaps of progress—small steps will do just fine. And with each small step, I pat myself on the back.

*Catch yourself doing something right. Any little thing ... every little thing.* Reach your right hand over your left shoulder and pat yourself on the back. Say, "Way to go! You did well!" Because you did.

(In case you're wondering, today—some 20 years later—my friend Kathryn is fit, trim, athletic, and a regular at the gym. She's in her 50s and has a body that many 30-year-olds would envy!)

*When it is obvious that the goal cannot be reached, don't adjust the goal, adjust the action steps.*

≈ *Confucius, Chinese philosopher, teacher* ≈

How *do you* spell

# SUCCESS ...

**S** elf-acceptance and self-love

**U** nconditional love of family and friends

**C** ontribution and service to others

**C** ommitment to living in integrity

**E** xcellence in achievement

**S** erenity, Security, and Sanity about money

**S** piritual growth and inner peace

# It is *not* the mountain WE CONQUER, *but* ourselves.

≈ *Sir Edmund Hillary, first man to climb Mt. Everest* ≈

## HAPPINESS IS ...

# *Focusing on what you can do, not what you can't do.*

I AM ONLY ONE, BUT I AM ONE.
I CANNOT DO EVERYTHING, BUT I CAN DO SOMETHING.
AND I WILL NOT LET WHAT I CANNOT DO INTERFERE
WITH WHAT I CAN DO.

*≈ Edward Everett Hale ≈*

# LOSING WEIGHT

## *By* BJ GALLAGHER

My friend Karen Cutts was a wise, loving woman. One day I was complaining to her about my problem sticking with my food plan, when she suggested, *"Don't let what you can't do stop you from what you can do."*

I asked her how that pertained to losing weight.

She explained: "Well, OK, you can't seem to give up sugar. Can you give up just one form of sugar?"

"Yes, I suppose I could give up ice cream," I replied. "Great!" she smiled. "Then do that. You can't give up all sugar but you can give up ice cream."

"Oh, I get it," I said. It made perfect sense—not just about eating, but about life.

"Don't let what you can't do stop you from what you can do" has become one of those simple guiding principles that helps me in so many of my daily activities. If I can't go biking because I live on a mountain, I CAN go hiking instead. If I can't play racquetball because

I twist my ankles easily, I CAN go swimming instead. If I can't afford to hire an expensive personal trainer, I CAN afford an exercise DVD to use at home. If I can't go to an expensive spa, I CAN take a long, luxurious bubble bath.

Karen's words helped me give up my limited thinking, which had been a huge impediment to my own self-care. Now I do what I can, when I can, as often as I can. Just because I can't do everything doesn't mean I can't do something.

# "YES"

## IS CONTAGIOUS ON A SUBLIMINAL LEVEL. IT AFFECTS EVERYTHING YOU DO.

≈ *SARK, artist, author* ≈

# Circles of
# INFLUENCE

Years ago, Steve Covey wrote a hugely popular book called *The Seven Habits of Highly Effective People*. It contained many practical, effective tips and tools to help people become more effective in their lives. My favorite tool is one I use almost daily in my own life and I've shared it with countless others in my seminars and speeches. It's called Circles of Influence. I've altered it slightly from Covey's original version—but I don't think he'll mind.

*Visualize a target in your mind*—or draw one on a piece of paper. This target is just two concentric circles, the smaller one inside the larger one. The small circle—the bull's eye—represents the things you can control in your life. It's small because, when you think about it, you really can't control very much. You can't control other people, including your spouse and kids; you can't control the job market; you can't control your boss, coworkers, the economy, Congress, the weather, traffic on your local roads, and much more. The one thing you CAN control is yourself, and maybe a few other things. So put yourself in the center circle, along with anything else you think you can control.

The second circle, the larger one, represents all the things (and people) you can influence, but not control. For instance, you probably have considerable influence on your friends and family. Maybe you have some influence at work. You have influence in your community because you can get involved and help make good things happen. You can even influence the federal government—

by voting, signing petitions and sending emails, calling your elected representatives, and more. So put the people and things you can influence in this larger circle.

Now, anything that is NOT inside these two circles is something over which you have NO control and NO influence. I've mentioned some of these already: weather, traffic, the economy, your company being bought out, a department merger, getting laid off from your job, and more. You get the idea.

> There is only one way to happiness and that is **TO CEASE WORRYING** about things which are beyond the power of our will.
>
> *Epictetus, Greek philosopher*

Now, here's the point: Highly effective people are those who focus all their time and energy on what's INSIDE these two circles—they focus on what they CAN control and what they CAN influence. They spend NO time or energy on anything OUTSIDE the circles—they don't waste a moment of precious time on stuff they can't control or influence. And that, in a nutshell, is how people become highly effective.

I would also add that this is also how people become happy. They focus their attention on things they can do something about and they don't waste time, attention, and energy on things they can't do anything about.

### *Want to be happy?*
### *Keep your focus on the bull's eye.*

# USEFULNESS IS HAPPINESS,

and … all other things are but incidental.

*≈ Lydia Maria Child, author ≈*

## HAPPINESS IS ...

# *Freedom from perfectionism.*

THE THING THAT IS REALLY HARD, AND REALLY AMAZING,
IS GIVING UP ON BEING PERFECT
AND BEGINNING THE WORK OF BECOMING YOURSELF.

*≈ Anna Quindlen, journalist, author ≈*

# *Daily* AFFIRMATIONS *for*
# REAL PEOPLE

*by* RHODA GROSSMAN

The other night I sat on the couch in a spaghetti-splattered sweat suit attempting to internalize my daily affirmation—*"I will radiate beauty from within"*—when the phone rang. It was my girlfriend. The first words out of her mouth were, "I just burst the seam on a pair of pants I was trying on in the fitting room." Her pants-splitting-in-the-fitting-room story automatically reminded

me of my jammed-zipper-in-the-ladies-room-of-the-fancy-restaurant story, which in turn led her to recount how she once spent five out of six dinner courses with a piece of arugula stuck on her tooth. It was as we sat on the phone revealing our most humiliating moments to one another that I had a revelation about what inspires us: *Affirmations are nice. But what's really moving to women are hideous admissions.*

Which makes you feel better? The book's affirmation: "No matter how high the mountain, today I will climb it," or the friend's admission: "I shut the office door, fell asleep on the computer keyboard and shorted out the system by drooling on the ENTER button."

Which gives you a better grasp on reality? The book's affirmation: "I will revel in who I am, not in who others expect me to be," or the friend's admission: "I combined seven microwaveable ravioli dinners into a ceramic bowl and tried to pretend it was my family's secret recipe at the school potluck."

Which thought is more comforting? The book's affirmation: *"I will conduct my life on a higher plane and will not allow myself to be consumed by pettiness,"* or the friend's admission: "I spent 14 hours searching for a pair of earrings to go with my new outfit."

> *Being happy doesn't mean that everything is perfect. It means that you've decided to look beyond the imperfections.*
>
> *Anonymous*

To hear a friend's admission is to know that there's another person in the world who has stooped just as low, if not lower, than you. There's solace in knowing that someone else went for a power walk and wound up at the ice cream store. There's inspiration in hearing that someone else not only stores her financial records in paper bags, but once accidentally gave them all to Goodwill.

Over the weekend a table full of dinner guests sat waiting in the dining room as I frantically raced around the kitchen trying to repair my rubberized chicken cacciatore and runny spinach soufflé. Instead of reciting my affirmation for the day, *"I am bigger than all of my problems combined,"* suddenly all I could think of was my friend's admission, "I once set the curtains on fire with my flaming peaches in front of 15 people." Ha! I thought, empowered by her failure. I'm about to be humiliated, but at least I'm not alone. With that I grabbed my platters of ruined food and marched through the dining room doors to face my guests. On second thought, maybe the most affirming thing we can tell ourselves every day is this: I will make time to call a girlfriend today and talk.

# THE CHIPPED CUP

*by* BJ Gallagher

*While having my morning tea today*
        *I noticed that my favorite cup was chipped.*
              *And I wanted to throw it away.*

*It's not that it was such a big chip—not really.*
        *It's more like a small, tea-stained,*
           *crescent-shaped crack,*
               *just inside the lip of the cup.*

*In fact, you can't even see it*
            *from the outside.*

*But the chip still bothers me.*
        *I don't like things that are damaged and flawed—*
        *I want them perfect.*

*That cup is a lot like me—*
      *chipped,*
          *cracked,*
             *stained,*
               *and imperfect.*
    *And I want to throw ME away.*

My imperfections seem glaring (even if others don't see them).
I try hard to be
        kind and generous,
                patient and thoughtful,
        compassionate and caring.

But every day—
        every hour—
                I fall short.

I want so much to be perfect—and I'm not.
        Tears of disappointment well up.
                I take my sadness
                        to meditation.

And in my quiet time
        the wise words of a good friend
                come to me:
                "God doesn't make junk."

I open my eyes and see the trees…
                with their crooked branches, rough bark,
        and lack of proper pruning.
They are perfect in their imperfection.

*(continued)*

I look around at the plants and flowers…
with their uneven growth,
lopsided blossoms,
and bugs on their leaves.
They, too, are perfect in their imperfection.

I look at the clouds,
the mountains,
the shoreline,
and the skyline.
I see that they are all perfectly imperfect.

Then I pick up my teacup—
cracked,
chipped,
and stained—
and now I see that it is perfectly imperfect, too.
So I think I'll keep it.

In nature, nothing is perfect and

# EVERYTHING
## IS PERFECT.

Trees can be contorted, bent in weird
ways, and they're still beautiful.

≈ *Alice Walker, author* ≈

# HAPPINESS IS ...

## *Self-Acceptance.*

I FEEL THAT WHEN WE REALLY LOVE AND ACCEPT
AND APPROVE OF OURSELVES EXACTLY AS WE ARE,
THEN EVERYTHING IN LIFE WORKS.

*≈ Louise Hay, spiritual teacher and author ≈*

# SELF-ESTEEM *versus* SELF-ACCEPTANCE

## *by* LEON SELTZER, PHD.

❃

*Though related, self-acceptance is not the same as self-esteem.* Whereas self-esteem refers specifically to how valuable, or worthwhile, we see ourselves, self-acceptance alludes to a far more global affirmation of self. When we're self-accepting, we're able to embrace all facets of ourselves—not just the positive, more "esteem-able" parts. As such, self-acceptance is unconditional, free of all qualification. We can recognize our weaknesses, limitations and foibles, but this awareness doesn't interfere with our ability to fully accept ourselves.

I regularly tell my therapy clients that if they genuinely want to improve their self-esteem, they need to explore what parts of themselves they're not yet able to accept. Ultimately, liking ourselves more (or getting on better terms with ourselves) has mostly to do with self-acceptance. And it's only when we stop judging ourselves that we can secure a more positive sense of who we are. Which is why I believe our self-esteem rises naturally as soon as we stop being so hard on ourselves. And it's precisely because self-acceptance involves far more than self-esteem that it's generally seen (as self-esteem is not) to be crucial to our happiness and peace of mind.

*~ Source: Psychology Today, Sept. 9, 2008*

# ENOUGH *by* BJ Gallagher

It's a familiar tune running through my head …
## "Not *pretty* enough."
## "Not *talented* enough."
## "Not *thin* enough."
## "Not *smart* enough."
## The chorus sings,
## "*Not* enough! *Not* enough! *Not* enough!"

They're an a cappella group—
the voices of Insecurity,
Unworthiness, and Self-doubt—
warbling their anxious refrain.
Sometimes Self-hatred joins in for a downbeat jam session.
I'm tired of their same old tune—
"Not enough" on an endless loop.
How can I muffle their voices?
Or get them to sing a new tune?
Oh, there they go again—do you hear them, too?
"Not enough,
not enough,
not enough …"
## Please, ENOUGH already!

I have never seen a person

# GROW OR CHANGE

in a self-constructive meaningful way when …
motivated by guilt, shame, or self-hate.

*≈ Herb Goldberg, therapist, author ≈*

If you make friends with yourself
you will never be alone.

*Maxwell Maltz*

It is the chiefest point
of happiness that a man is
willing to be what he *is*.

≈ *Desiderius Erasmus* ≈

## HAPPINESS IS ...

# *Making peace with the past.*

WE CAN NEVER MAKE PEACE IN THE OUTER WORLD
UNTIL WE MAKE PEACE WITH OURSELVES.

*≈ HH the Dalai Lama ≈*

# BLAME YOUR PARENTS *for the way you are ...*
# BLAME YOURSELF *if you stay that way*

*by* BJ GALLAGHER

❋

***Have you ever heard someone say something so simple and yet so profound that you were stunned at the truth of her statement? Have you ever experienced a revelation, an epiphany, as the result of a simple bit of human insight or wisdom?***

That was my reaction when my mother made this statement to me one day: "Blame your parents for the way you are; blame yourself if you stay that way." At that time I had been complaining a lot about the parenting I had received from my folks. In my opinion, they were too strict, controlling, perfectionist, rigid, and so on. I viewed myself as the  helpless victim of their less-than-enlightened parenting practices. I felt that the problems I had as an adult were the direct result of the dysfunctional family in which I grew up ... or so I thought. I had plenty of blame to heap upon my mom and dad.

Then one day, in the middle of one of my grievance litanies, my mother turned to me and said simply, "Blame your parents for the way you are; blame yourself if you stay that way." Then she turned back to washing the dishes.

The statement was like a glass of cold water in my face. If I had had my wits about me, I should have said, "Thanks, Mom, I needed that." But I didn't have my wits about me. I was stunned into silence.

Today I am grateful for my mother's comment. It took me a while to come to grips with the enormity of it … I had to digest and reflect upon the implications of her message. She was right. ***I could, indeed, blame my parents for the mistakes they had made and the kind of person I grew up to be.*** Nothing in her statement implied that my parents were not accountable for their actions.

But I also had a choice. I could choose to continue to wallow in victimhood and blame the past for my problems today. Or, I could take responsibility for my present and my future—I could choose to change.

I can make the Popeye defense: "I yam what I yam," and resign myself to the fact that "character is fate." ***Or, I can take the stance that human beings can change—sometimes rather dramatically.***

Today, I am a work in progress, and my future is limited only by my own beliefs and my willingness to forgive, heal, grow, stretch and learn. Mom was right …

I have *only* myself to blame
if I stay stuck in the past.

# ❧ FAMILY MEMORIES ❧

## by Carmen Ruiz

I guess I was complaining, but didn't even realize it. My mother and I were doing dishes and I was telling her how I felt about our Easter together. It was lovely spending the day with her and her second husband and his children, but deep inside me a little voice kept whispering, "If only Papa were here, the holiday would be complete."

When I told her this, she looked at me with that tough-love look of hers and said, *"You need to accept the fact that our family is never going to be the way it was before."*

I didn't say anything. I wiped my hands on a towel and left the kitchen.

On my way home that evening, the truth hit me: What I really needed to do was accept the fact that my family never was the way I wanted them to be … even when Mama and Papa were together! I was still clinging to a fantasy family in my head—a family that never existed.

Mama was right: I needed to let go of the hope of us being one big happy family again someday. I needed to accept my family as they were—both my past family and my present one. A hard dose of reality, but an important one.

Set *peace of mind* as your highest goal and organize your life around it.

≈ *Brian Tracy, author, speaker* ≈

❈

HAPPINESS IS ...

# *Accepting others just as they are ... and just as they aren't.*

IF YOU JUDGE PEOPLE, YOU HAVE NO TIME
TO LOVE THEM.

≈ *Mother Teresa, humanitarian* ≈

# TRUST PEOPLE
## *to be* WHO THEY ARE

❋

Years ago, I heard a great story that prompted me to re-think the whole no-tion of trust. No one knows the source of this story, though some misattribute it to Aesop. But whoever wrote it was very wise. See if you think so, too:

*One day, a scorpion looked around at the mountain where he lived and decided that he wanted a change. So he set out on a journey through the forests and hills. He climbed over rocks and under vines and kept going until he reached a stream.*

*The stream was wide and deep, and the scorpion stopped to reconsider the situa-tion. He couldn't see any way across. He walked upstream for a bit and then back downstream, looking for a way to get across to the other side. He came upon a frog sitting in the rushes by the bank of the stream.*

*"Hellooo, Mr. Frog!" the scorpion said in his nicest voice, "Would you be so kind as to give me a ride on your back across the stream?"*

*"Well now, Mr. Scorpion! How do I know that if I try to help you, you won't sting me?" asked the frog.*

*"I would never do that," the scorpion replied. "If I sting you, then you would drown and I would drown along with you, for I cannot swim."*

Now this made sense to the frog, but he was still suspicious. "Yes, that's true, but how do I know you won't sting me anyway?"

"I would have to be crazy to do that," the scorpion reassured him. "I don't want to die. I just want to get to the other side of the stream."

"You've got a point there," said the frog as he mulled it over.

Finally the frog agreed to take the scorpion across the river. "OK, I'll take you across. Hop on my back and we'll get going. Just be careful with your stinger."

"Sure, sure, of course," the scorpion replied.

He crawled onto the frog's back and the frog slid into the river. The water swirled around them, but the frog stayed near the surface so the scorpion would not drown. He kicked strongly through the stream, his webbed feet paddling surely and steadily against the current.

But about halfway across the stream, the frog suddenly felt a sharp sting in his back. A deadening numbness began to creep into his limbs.

"What have you done?" croaked the frog, looking back over his shoulder at his passenger. "Why on earth did you sting me? Now we're both going to drown!"

"I couldn't help myself," the scorpion shrugged as he sank with the frog. "It's just my nature."

When people talk about trust, they say things like: "*I don't trust him,*" or "*Can she be trusted?*" or "*I wouldn't trust him as far as I can throw him.*"

But because of this story, I think of trust in a different way: I trust people to be who they are. I trust them to behave in keeping with their character.

If one of my coworkers is a snake in the grass, I expect him to act like a snake in the grass and deal with him accordingly. It doesn't mean I refuse to work with him; it just means I recognize who I'm dealing with and take appropriate steps to protect myself. I don't have to like him —but I do have to work with him.

> I have learned silence from the talkative, toleration from the intolerant, kindness from the unkind. Yet, strange, I am ungrateful to these teachers.
>
> *Khalil Gibran,*
> *Lebanese-born poet, author*

Or if my friend is flakey and disorganized, I don't have to stop being her friend. If I like her anyway, I simply accept the way she is and make sure that her flakiness doesn't have a negative impact on me. I trust her to be flakey.

"The Scorpion and the Frog" taught me to trust people to act in accordance with who they are … and who they aren't. My life's been a lot happier ever since.

*A slight, a snotty remark or a flake-out—*
*they aren't necessarily a reflection of our friend's*
*affection towards us or of their degree of*
*caring. It's just a reflection of who they are.*

≈ *Debbie Puente, examiner.com Los Angeles* ≈

# LENSES LIMITED

*by* BJ Gallagher

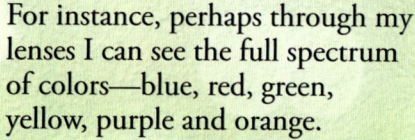

Imagine a world in which everyone
is issued a pair of glasses at birth.

No one thinks anything about it—
it's absolutely normal.

These glasses all appear to be the same,
so people assume they are.

They assume that the world they see
through their own lenses is the same
world that everyone else sees.

But alas, everyone's glasses are not the
same. They are each just a little bit different from one another.

For instance, perhaps through my
lenses I can see the full spectrum
of colors—blue, red, green,
yellow, purple and orange.

Through your lenses you can see
only black and white.

Depending on what we're looking at in the world, we might see
something quite different from
each other—
even though we're looking
at the same object or situation.

Since I see in Technicolor,
I will describe what I see through
my lenses.

Since you see in black and white,
you will describe what you see
through yours.

And then we argue about who
is correct.

We get upset because
we each know that we're right—
and we can't understand
why the other person
doesn't see it the way we do.

It's all because of those glasses.

*What can we do
to keep our glasses from
becoming blinders?*

*We can share …*
"This is what I see through my
lenses."

*We can ask …*
"How does it look through
your lenses?"

*We can strive to understand …*
"Tell me more."

*We can listen and learn,
discuss and discover,
explore and explain.*

*We can look for common
ground …* and still appreciate
uncommon differences.

# Let's not let our lenses *limit* our lives.

If there were in the world today any large number of people who *desired their own happiness more* than they desired the unhappiness of others, we could have paradise in a few years.

≈ *Bertrand Russell, philosopher* ≈

❊

## HAPPINESS IS ...

# *Keeping expectations to a minimum.*

MOST PEOPLE ASK FOR HAPPINESS
ON CONDITION.
HAPPINESS CAN ONLY BE FELT
IF YOU DON'T SET ANY CONDITIONS.

*≈ Artur Rubenstein ≈*

# NO EXPECTATIONS

*by* BJ GALLAGHER

❋

A few years ago, I made a coffee date with my good friend, Dr. Arnold Chanin. We agreed to meet early one Saturday morning at a coffee shop convenient for both of us.

When I walked into the coffee shop, Arnie looked up from his newspaper and his face lit up when he saw me. He jumped to his feet and opened his arms to give me a big hug.

*"What a wonderful surprise!" he exclaimed as he hugged me. "I am so happy to see you!"*

"Arnie," I replied, "We have a coffee date, remember?"

"Oh yes," he said as he sat down. "I remember."

"Then why are you surprised?" I asked.

"Do you know how many people make appointments and then don't show up?" he asked. "It happens all the time. So I have learned not to have any expectations. That way, if they don't show up, I'm not upset—and if they do show up, I'm surprised and delighted."

"Well, that's a novel attitude," I marveled.

"Hey, what can I say?" Arnie replied. "It makes me happy."

# RESENTMENTS
## UNDER CONSTRUCTION
*by BJ Gallagher*

Someone wise once told me
    that expectations are simply
        resentments waiting to happen.

I've learned the hard way
    how true this is.

A friend disappoints me
    and I'm hurt and angry.
Resentment bubbles up inside
and I have a bitter taste in my mouth.
I want to complain and protest
    the disappointment I've suffered.

So, how long do I carry
    my disappointment and resentment?

Not long,
if I'm smart.

For holding onto a resentment
is like swallowing poison
and hoping the other person will die.

I must let it go—
forgive and move on—
for my own sake
as well as theirs.

And in the future,
I must try my best to remember
to let go of expectations
and love my friends
just as they are—
not how I want them to be.

When I was in grade school,
they told me to write down
what I wanted to be when I grew up.

I wrote down, "HAPPY."

They told me I didn't
understand the assignment.
I told them they
didn't understand life.

≈ Anonymous ≈

Nothing can bring you happiness but

# YOURSELF.

*≈ Ralph Waldo Emerson, poet, essayist ≈*

## HAPPINESS IS ...

# *Not taking things personally.*

ABOUT ALL YOU CAN DO IN LIFE IS BE WHO YOU ARE.
SOME PEOPLE WILL LOVE YOU FOR YOU.
MOST WILL LOVE YOU FOR WHAT YOU CAN DO FOR
THEM, AND SOME WON'T LIKE YOU AT ALL.

*≈ Rita Mae Brown, novelist ≈*

# YOUR PEOPLE

*By* CHELLIE CAMPBELL

❈

*As I've gone through life, I've been greatly influenced by wonderful self-help books by marvelous teachers, giving me life lessons in moments of illumination.* One such moment came from a passage in Wayne Dyer's book, *Your Erroneous Zones*, where he reminds us that half of the people in the world aren't going to like you, and there's nothing you can do about it.

I was shocked. It was definitely an "Aha!" moment. I had been raised to be a good girl, a people-pleaser, always trying to make sure people around me were happy and that I didn't offend anyone with any statement or act. What an impossible task! I was doomed to failure, and I became nervous and unhappy when I couldn't please everyone. I was one of those people who would go to a party, find 99 people out 100 liked me, but follow around the one who didn't, trying to change his mind.

*How much money is lost in life by people chasing people who don't like them, trying to make them happy?* It can be a boss, a client, or a family member. This person clearly isn't one of Your People. Let them go! You will never please them, satisfy them, or measure up to their vision of how you ought to be. You'll make yourself crazy spending any time or effort on them.

*Look for Your People—pick them to be on your team.* When someone asks me how you can tell who they are, I tell them it's easy: *you know Your people because you like them—immediately.* And they like you back. Just listen to your gut instinct, your feelings. You can tell them from the chemistry that flows between you, the quickening interest in their eyes, the body language that tells you they're awake and listening. They have praise for you, your products or services, your ideas. If they are a client or a boss, they pay you well.

The Other People have "out of body" experiences around you. You know how this happens when you're talking to them and their eyes glaze over and you know mentally, they just left the room. *Or some anger surfaces in the conversation, they take offense to something you said, or disagree strongly with your core values.* They never think you're good enough; they put you down; they "should" on you. If they're a boss or a client, they will never be happy with your performance; they will niggle you to death over the smallest of details; and they won't pay you what you're worth—if they pay you at all! Instead of buy-buy, say bye-bye!

*Source: The Wealthy Spirit, by Chellie Campbell*

*Don't take anything personally.*
Nothing others do is because of you.
What others say and do is a projection
of their own reality, their own dream.
When you are immune to the opinions
and actions of others, you won't be a
victim of needless suffering.

*≈ Don Miguel Ruiz, The Four Agreements ≈*

# IT'S NOT ABOUT
# YOU

*by* Mac Anderson

One of the most common ways we get in the way of our own happiness is by taking things personally when they're not personal at all. So many people seem to be sensitive creatures—taking affront at being "disrespected," jumping to conclusions that someone else is being "rude," and quick to outrage over any perceived slight.

Here's a common example: You call a friend on the phone but he's not there, so you leave a voicemail message. Hours roll by and your friend doesn't call you back. The day ends and still no call. Where does your mind go? If you're like most people, you wonder, "Why hasn't he called me back?"

Another day goes by and still no call. Now you're worried, "What's wrong? Why hasn't he returned my call? I wonder if something happened to him?"

A week goes by and still no call. Now you're furious. "What a jerk! The least he could do is return my call!"

The conversation in your head may be slightly different, depending on who you're waiting to hear from—but it's always negative. When someone doesn't call you back, you think something negative about yourself ("He must be mad at me," or "He doesn't like me.") or you think something negative about the

> We also often add to our pain and suffering by
> being overly sensitive, over-reacting to minor things,
> and sometimes taking things too personally.
>
> *Tenzin Gyatso, the Dalai Lama*

other person ("He's rude," or "He's a jerk," or worse.) Either way, you let your happiness be diminished by your interpretation of someone else's behavior.

The truth is, you have no idea why your friend hasn't called! He could be out of town; he might be ill or injured; he could be up to his ears in work; he might be on a tight deadline with no time to call; perhaps his voicemail isn't working and he never got your message; or maybe he simply forgot to call. There are a hundred possible reasons why he didn't call—reasons that have nothing to do with you!

*Here's a simple, effective happiness tip: Don't take things personally. Don't speculate on why people do things until you have actual facts; don't attach meanings to events until you know the whole story; don't make up stories in lieu of real information.*

All that happened is your friend didn't promptly return your call. That's all.

You can free yourself from hurt feelings, misunderstandings, and crossed communications by simply noticing what happened (or didn't happen)—but NOT attaching any meaning to it. You'll find freedom and happiness that way.

## HAPPINESS IS ...

# *Freedom from concern about what others think of you.*

DON'T RELY ON SOMEONE ELSE FOR YOUR HAPPINESS AND SELF-WORTH. ONLY YOU CAN BE RESPONSIBLE FOR THAT. IF YOU CAN'T LOVE AND RESPECT YOURSELF, NO ONE ELSE WILL BE ABLE TO MAKE THAT HAPPEN. ACCEPT WHO YOU ARE—COMPLETELY— THE GOOD AND THE BAD. AND MAKE CHANGES AS YOU SEE FIT— NOT BECAUSE SOMEONE ELSE WANTS YOU TO BE DIFFERENT.

≈ *Stacey Charter* ≈

## People Say The
# DARNDEST THINGS!

❄

French existential philosopher Jean Paul Sartre used to say, "Hell is other people." And we all know what he meant, don't we? People can be frustrating, annoying, irrational … and downright infuriating. "If only people would behave," we lament, "my life would be just fine!" or we mutter, *"The world would be a better place if other people would just shape up!"*

But they don't. People do what they do— for all kinds of reasons, some of which make sense, some of which make no sense at all. *Everyone marches to his or her own drummer, whether we like it or not.*

Wanting other people to "behave" or "shape up" can be a serious barrier to your own happiness … if you let it. If your happiness is dependent on others behaving in a certain way, you're in deep yogurt. Why? Because you can't control other people. You can only control yourself (and sometimes, I'll bet, you can't even do that). By hitching your happiness to someone else, you are guaranteeing yourself a life of never-ending disappointment, frustration and resentment.

What's worse is to make your happiness contingent upon other people's opinion of you! Have you ever done a good deed, only to have someone criticize you for it? Have you ever offered a helping hand, only to have the other person turn around and bite it? Have you ever accomplished something remarkable, only to have others dismiss it or try to tear it down? It hurts. It hurts a lot sometimes.

*The only solution is to unhook your happiness from other people and commit yourself to marching to your own drummer—regardless of what anyone else thinks or says. Easy to say, hard to do.*

It may sound paradoxical, but your happiness depends on you not depending upon others for your happiness. Detach from the tyranny of people's approval; detach from the slavery to others' opinions; stop bending over backwards to please everyone else. Then, and only then, can you claim your own happiness.

> It took me a
> long time
> 
> # NOT TO
> JUDGE MYSELF
> through someone
> else's eyes.
> 
> *Sally Field, actress*

Back in the late '60s, in his booklet for college student leaders, Kent Keith wrote a wise and useful list of commandments to help people *"find personal meaning in a crazy world."* It's one of the noblest, most inspiring, practical pieces of wisdom we've ever read, so we'd like to share it with you here. Read it and reap ... happiness!

# ANYWAY:
## The Paradoxical Commandments©

*by Dr. Kent M. Keith*

People are illogical, unreasonable, and self-centered.
*Love them anyway.*

If you do good, people will accuse you of selfish ulterior motives.
*Do good anyway.*

If you are successful, you will win false friends and true enemies.
*Succeed anyway.*

The good you do today will be forgotten tomorrow.
*Do good anyway.*

Honesty and frankness make you vulnerable.
*Be honest and frank anyway.*

The biggest men and women with the biggest ideas can be shot down by the smallest men and women with the smallest minds.
*Think big anyway.*

People favor underdogs but follow only top dogs.
*Fight for a few underdogs anyway.*

What you spend years building may be destroyed overnight.
*Build anyway.*

People really need help but may attack you if you do help them.
*Help people anyway.*

Give the world the best you have and you'll get kicked in the teeth.

## *Give the world the best you have anyway.*

# RISK! RISK ANYTHING!

Care no more for the opinions of others,
for those voices. Do the hardest thing on
earth for you. Act for yourself. Face the truth.

*≈ Katherine Mansfield, New Zealander writer ≈*

# OUT OF THE MOUTHS OF BABES
*by BJ Gallagher*

I've often suspected that my son Michael is a wise, old soul born into a young person's body. I sometimes think that this old soul came into my life to offer pearls of wisdom when I need them.

One weekend, when Michael was seven years old, he was preparing to go spend the weekend with his dad. He came out of his bedroom wearing a pair of blue jeans and a colorful T-shirt.

"Why don't you put on a shirt with a collar?" I suggested. "Like a polo shirt or something. I'll bet Daddy would really like that."

I had spent my own childhood trying to please my stern, perfectionist, military father … and now here I was, trying to train my son to please his own stern, perfectionist, corporate father.

*Upon hearing my suggestion, Michael looked up at me and said, "Mom, this is who I am. Either Daddy loves me in a T-shirt or he doesn't love me at all."*

How did he get so wise?

I felt about two inches tall. Of course he was right. That wise, old soul in a young body had just offered another one of those pearls of wisdom. I was humbled and grateful.

Today, if I could string together all the pearls of wisdom he has given me over the years, it would be a luminous strand of pearls beyond price. Time has made me older—Michael has made me wiser.

To be obliged to beg our

# DAILY HAPPINESS

from others bespeaks a more lamentable poverty than
that of him who begs his daily bread.

*≈ Charles Caleb Colton, English cleric and writer ≈*

## HAPPINESS IS ...

# *Forgiving and moving on with your life.*

TO FORGIVE IS TO SET A PRISONER FREE
AND DISCOVER THAT THE PRISONER WAS YOU.

*≈ Lewis Smedes, pastor, author ≈*

# *The* POWER *of*
# FORGIVENESS

❋

We all experience resentment: resentment when someone cheats us, resentment when we are accused or punished unjustly, resentment when someone doesn't treat us the way we want to be treated, resentment when life isn't fair, and so on. Having resentments isn't such a bad thing—it's a human thing. It's holding onto them that causes problems.

Years ago I saw an incredibly powerful picture in the newspaper. It was a picture of Pope John Paul II in the jail cell of the man who had tried to assassinate him. The Pope and his attacker were sitting face to face, both leaning forward, their heads almost touching. The Pope was holding the hands of the gunman, as if listening with great intensity to someone for whom he had affection. It was an intimate scene of two men engaged in a very personal conversation. Pope John Paul II had gone to visit his would-be assassin to forgive him, and the scene was their conversation of forgiveness and reconciliation. At the time, I didn't understand how such a scene could take place. It was unfathomable to me how anyone could forgive a person who had tried to kill him.

It is no accident that all the world's great religions emphasize the need for forgiveness. What great spiritual teachers know is that forgiveness helps the forgiver even more than it helps the forgiven. For as long as a person holds a resentment or grudge against another person, the person with the resentment suffers much more than the person who is the resented one.

> # FORGIVENESS
> does not change the past, but it does enlarge the future.
>
> *Paul Boese, Dutch botanist*

This is a strange paradox. We are angry at a person, so we punish them by staying angry, being resentful, perhaps even hating that person. Who are we really hurting with our vengeful anger? Are we hurting the person we want to hurt? Think about it. Whose body holds the anger? Whose jaw tightens? Whose fists clench? Whose blood boils? Whose mind is obsessed with thoughts of vengeance and retribution? Who loses sleep nursing their anger? Whose digestion is upset? So, who's really being hurt here? The person you're mad at ... or you?

Where does it get you to continue nursing your old wounds and resentments?

It keeps you a prisoner. You have no freedom when you are carrying the burden of anger and resentment.

Until you can forgive others (not forget—just forgive) and let go of your resentments, you cannot find lasting peace and happiness.

Resentments will poison you. Give them up.

*Forgiveness is a funny thing.*
*It warms the heart and cools the sting.*

≈ *William Arthur Ward, scholar, pastor, author* ≈

How do you find

# FORGIVENESS?

**F** eel your hurt

**O** pen your mind

**R** elease your anger

**G** ive love a chance

**I** nquire within your heart

**V** enture into dialogue

**E** mbrace the other person

**N** udge yourself to keep at it, even when you don't want to

**E** njoy new possibilities and freedom

**S** eek Divine guidance and help

**S** avor your new serenity and peace

## HAPPINESS IS ...

## *A choice.*

CHOICE IS A POWERFUL THING.
MORE OF ANYTHING OR EVERYTHING
WILL NOT MAKE A DIFFERENCE TO YOUR
HAPPINESS ... UNTIL YOU CONSCIOUSLY
CHOOSE TO BE HAPPY.

*≈ Dr. Robert Holden, British psychologist, author ≈*

# YOU BECOME *what you* THINK ABOUT

*by* MAC ANDERSON

❄

*A Native American elder walks slowly down the path. The leaves of the trees and the soft breeze protect him from the heat of the noonday sun. In his worn, calloused hand is the small, soft hand of his young grandson. The two walk in silence.*

*After a time the grandfather interrupts the silence. "Grandson," he begins, "there are two wolves fighting in my heart. One wolf is angry, vengeful, jealous and violent. The other wolf is peaceful, loving, compassionate and joyful."*

*The boy looks up at his grandfather and asks, "Which wolf will win the battle of your heart?"*

*The wise elder replies, "The one I feed."*

This simple story provides the essence of a happy and fulfilled life…You become what you think about. The words seem almost too simple to feel important. However, if you get it—if you truly understand their meaning— you can forever harness the power of a positive attitude … and a much happier life.

Simply stated, if we choose to think positive thoughts, we'll get positive results; if we think negative thoughts, we'll get negative results.

When I first heard Earl Nightingale's famous audio recording, *The Strangest Secret*, I was a sophomore in college and it changed my life forever. It is composed of approximately 5,000 words; and in those words I found more wisdom, more common sense and more inspiration than in anything I had ever heard. From that point on, I've used Nightingale's message to keep me focused and motivated in good times and in bad. And I'm not alone. The essay has inspired millions around the world. In fact, it was the first non-musical recording to sell over one million copies. Here's a brief excerpt...

*George Bernard Shaw said, "People are always blaming their circumstances for what they are. I don't believe in circumstances. The people who get on in this world are the people who get up and look for the circumstances they want, and if they can't find them, make them."*

*Now it stands to reason that a person who is thinking about a concrete and worthwhile goal is going to reach it, because that's what they're thinking about.*

## *And we become what we think.*

*Conversely, the person who has no goal, who doesn't know where they're going, and whose thoughts must therefore be thoughts of confusion, anxiety, fear and worry —their life becomes one of frustration, fear, anxiety and worry. And if they think about nothing ... they become nothing.*

*You become what you think about; this simple, but life-changing law, can forever change the way you think about life, in a very wonderful and positive way.*

*Very little is needed
to make a happy life;
it is all within yourself,
in your way of thinking.*

≈ *Marcus Aurelius, Roman emperor* ≈

# HAPPINESS IS A
# CHOICE

*"Most people are about as happy as they make up their minds to be,"* Abraham Lincoln once wrote. *I've long thought so, too. Happiness is a choice as much as anything—a choice of perception, a choice of attitude, a choice of how you respond to life, a choice of action.*

One of my all-time favorite books is *Happiness is a Choice*, by Barry Neil Kaufman. Barry and his wife had a baby boy, their third child, who was diagnosed as autistic. At first, the couple was devastated—they thought their lives were ruined and their child doomed to a hopeless future.

But once they worked through their initial reaction to the diagnosis, they made a huge decision: they chose to be happy. They said, "We can let this situation drag us into depression and self-pity, OR we can decide to love our child, make a nurturing family for him, and have a good life together. They chose the latter.

They rejected the advice of doctors who told them to put the child in an institution and move on with their lives. Instead, they completely redesigned their home and their lives to meet the needs of their autistic toddler. He couldn't meet them in their world, so they met him in his. They sat on the floor and played with him, mimicking his shrieks, whoops, and wild gestures.

Bit by bit, they were able to build rapport with their son, teach him new behaviors, and coax him further and further into normalcy. The boy grew and thrived under his parents' unconditional love, patience, and teaching—it was a long, challenging process, but he graduated from high school, then college, with honors. And throughout those challenging years, Barry Neil Kaufman and his wife simply chose to be happy.

*We deem those happy who,*
*from the experience of life,*
*have learned to bear its ills,*
*without being overcome by them.*

≈ *Juvenal, first century Roman poet* ≈

# HAPPINESS IS ...

## *Sharing and giving.*

THOUSANDS OF CANDLES CAN BE LIT FROM A SINGLE
CANDLE, AND THE LIFE OF THE CANDLE WILL
NOT BE SHORTENED. HAPPINESS NEVER DECREASES
BY BEING SHARED.

≈ *The Buddha* ≈

# GIVE 'TIL IT HURTS

*by* BJ GALLAGHER

❄

Reverend Ed Bacon of All Saints Episcopal Church in Pasadena, California, stood at his pulpit, resplendent in his flowing white robe and colorful vestments. He's a big man with a booming voice and enough charisma to light up the sanctuary without candles. On this particular Sunday, he was practically glowing with joy—energized by his guest of honor, Archbishop Desmond Tutu, the Nobel Prize-winning peacemaker from South Africa.

*"Most people say, 'Give 'til it hurts,'" Reverend Ed announced to the standing-room-only congregation. "But I say, 'Give 'til it feels good!'"*

The crowd's laughter and applause thundered their approval. The choir burst into song as ushers made their way down the aisles with collection baskets.

This wasn't just any Sunday—and it wasn't just any collection. Archbishop Tutu had come to All Saints to tell us about the latest developments in his homeland. Apartheid had been abolished and the country was now embarking on the long, slow, painful journey of healing. A Truth and Reconciliation Commission (TRC) had been established to facilitate the healing process. It was a court-like body, chaired by Archbishop Tutu, which played a key role in the transition of South Africa to a full and free democracy. Anyone who felt

> You make a living by
> WHAT YOU GET
> but you make a life by
> WHAT YOU GIVE.
>
> *Anonymous*

that he or she had been a victim of apartheid's violence could come forward and be heard. Perpetrators of violence could also give testimony and request amnesty and forgiveness.

But, as Reverend Ed pointed out to us that Sunday morning, justice isn't free. It costs money to hold tribunals, to handle the paperwork, to underwrite the process of hearings and all the administrative details. So he asked the congregation to dig deep into our pockets and purses, since he was giving all the donations that Sunday to Archbishop Tutu to help support the ongoing work of the Truth and Reconciliation Commission.

"I've never done this before," Reverend Ed said, "But I'm going to do it today. I am urging to give what you can, in whatever form you can. If you want to donate your car, we'll take the pink slip. If you want to donate jewelry, we'll take that. If you want to give cash or a check, or even put your donation on a credit card, fine. We'll take it all. We here in Southern California have a wonderful standard of living—we're rich by any standard. So I'm asking you to give as much as you can to the people of South Africa to support their healing and reconciliation. *Most people say, 'Give until it hurts'—but I say, 'Give until it feels good!'*"

There wasn't a dry eye in the place. We were so moved by Tutu's sermon, so inspired by his moral authority and loving compassion, that we could do no less than give our all.

As the collection basket made its way toward me, I wondered what to do. My business had been slow, so I had no extra money to give. I needed my car, so I couldn't donate that. What can I give? I asked myself. I desperately wanted to support this marvelous process unfolding in South Africa. I wanted to contribute something—no matter how small—to the good people half-way around the world.

The collection basket finally came to me and I looked down into it, still not sure what to do. As my hands cradled the basket of love offerings, *I noticed that I was wearing a 14K gold and garnet ring my mother had given me on my 12th birthday.* Instantly, I knew what to do. I took off the ring, put it in the little white offering envelope, and dropped the envelope into the collection basket. Tears of joy streamed down my face as I passed the basket to the person next to me. I imagined the South Africans melting down my gold ring to help pay for their national healing. I was filled with gratitude and happiness to be a tiny part of something so momentous, so important, so essential to humanity.

As I wiped away my tears and joined the choir in song, I realized that Reverend Ed had been right. I gave … and it felt good.

*If you can't feed a
    hundred people,
then feed just one.*

≈ *Mother Teresa, humanitarian* ≈

# GIVING

*by* BJ Gallagher

"It's better to give than receive,"
   my mother used to say.
     But it took some years
of experience
     before I fully understood
      what she meant.

When I gave my subway seat
   to an old lady,
   **I felt kind.**

When I dropped a dollar
   into the street musician's hat,
   **I felt generous.**

When I let the harried driver
   cut in front of me on the road,
   **I felt patient.**

When I lent a hand
   to someone at work,
   **I felt a part of the team.**

When I brought a meal
   to my grieving neighbor,
   **I felt empathetic.**

When I gave some water
   to a thirsty dog,
   **I felt happy.**

When I wrote a check
   to a worthy cause,
   **I felt virtuous.**

When I gave my friend
   the benefit of the doubt,
   **I felt compassionate.**

I discovered that
when I give my time,
   my attention,
   my money,
   my thoughtfulness
to another—
   **I feel wonderful.**

Mom was right …
it **IS** better to give
than receive.

In giving,
*we generate warmth;*
in giving,
*we feel connected;*
in giving,
*we discover love.*

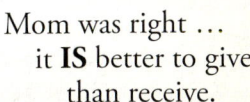

Happiness *is*

# GENEROUS ...

**G** iving with no strings attached

**E** xpecting nothing in return

**N** oticing what others need and want

**E** xercising your imagination and creativity in giving

**R** ealizing that "what goes around, comes around"

**O** pening your home as well as your heart

**U** nderstanding that it is the giver who is most enriched

**S** haring your time, attention, energy, money, and love

## HAPPINESS IS ...

# *A spiritual connection to the world.*

**HAPPINESS CANNOT BE TRAVELED TO, OWNED, EARNED, WORN OR CONSUMED. HAPPINESS IS THE SPIRITUAL EXPERIENCE OF LIVING EVERY MINUTE WITH LOVE, GRACE AND GRATITUDE.**

*≈ Denis Waitley, inspirational author, speaker ≈*

# DOG IS GOOD

## by BJ GALLAGHER

❄

*My dog Fannie is not a lap dog, nor is she one of those snuggly pooches who wants to crawl under the covers and sleep with me at night. She is soft, blonde, and fluffy—and looks like she would be a cuddly mutt—but she's not. Instead, she behaves like a guard dog.*

In the daytime, Fannie likes to hang out on the dog bed on our front porch or lie in the driveway and catch a few rays. At night, she'll sleep at the foot of my bed, on the floor in a dog bed, in the hallway on the rug, or by the front door. She moves from place to place throughout the night—but always positions herself somewhere between me and the front door, as if she is on patrol. She acts as if it is her job to protect me from any danger that might come from outside.

Sometimes in the early morning hours before dawn, I'll wake up and see where Fannie is sleeping. I creep out of bed, scoop her up in my arms, and take her back to bed for a cuddle. I get into spooning position with her and bury my face in the thick fur on the back of her neck. Her head is cradled in the crook of my left arm and my right arm is draped over her, with my hand gently rubbing her belly. She falls back to sleep immediately, with the softest, gentlest little snore I've ever heard.

As I lie there listening to her breathe, feeling the warmth of her body next to mine, with my face buried in her fur, I am flooded with happiness. I feel deeply connected to my dog, to all living creatures, to the Universe, and to God. I offer a prayer of joyful gratitude: "God, you can take me now … It doesn't get any better than this. If I died right this minute, it's OK with me. I'm a happy woman."

God hasn't taken me up on my offer yet, so I continue to enjoy as many of those sleepy dog mornings as I can. Dog is good.

*Happiness is a butterfly,*
*which, when pursued, is always just beyond your grasp,*
*but which, if you sit down quietly, may alight upon you.*

*≈ Nathaniel Hawthorne, novelist ≈*

Happiness *is*

# SERENITY ...

**S** elflessness

**E** go-reduction

**R** eal Peace of Mind

**E** njoying Simple Pleasures

**N** o Drama

**I** nterest in Others

**T** ranquility

**Y** es to God's Grace and Love

Benjamin Franklin pointed out that

## "The U. S. Constitution doesn't guarantee happiness, only the pursuit of it. You have to catch up to it yourself."

We agree. And we hope that the "21 Rules for Living a Happy Life" we have shared with you will help you catch up to happiness. As our final gift to you, we're concluding with

### "THE HAPPINESS CREED."

We invite you to copy it on a 3x5 card and carry it with you in your wallet; share it with your friends and family; tape it to your bathroom mirror; post it on your Facebook page; put it in places where you will see it often – and remind yourself to simply...

# "CHOOSE TO BE HAPPY."

Happiness is your spiritual DNA ...
Joy is the organic state of your soul.
It is not something you achieve;
it is something you accept.

≈ *Dr. Robert Holden,*
  *British psychologist, author* ≈

# THE **HAPPINESS** CREED

*by* BJ Gallagher

*I believe that happiness is my birthright,*
*as well as my responsibility;*
**and I commit to claiming it.**

*I believe that happiness is here and now;*
**and I commit to awakening to it.**

*I believe that happiness is a choice;*
**and I commit to choosing it.**

*I believe that happiness is a habit;*
**and I commit to cultivating it.**

*I believe that happiness is free,*
*like rainbows, sunshine, and air;*
**and I commit to reveling in it.**

*I believe that happiness is always available,*
*no matter what others are doing;*
**and I commit to creating it.**

*I believe that happiness is an inside job,*
*not dependent on money, fame, or possessions;*
**and I commit to living it.**

*I believe that happiness is an attitude of gratitude;*
**and I commit to giving thanks.**

*I believe that happiness is in action;*
**and I commit to generating it.**

*I believe that happiness is contagious;*
**and I commit to sharing it.**

*I believe that happiness is a prayer,*
*uniting me with the universe;*
**and I commit to offering it.**

*I believe that happiness is my calling —*

**I must be the happiness
I wish to see in the world.**

# MAC ANDERSON

MAC ANDERSON is the founder of Simple Truths and Successories, Inc., the leader in designing and marketing products for motivation and recognition. These companies, however, are not the first success stories for Mac. He was also the founder and CEO of McCord Travel, the largest travel company in the Midwest, and part owner/VP of sales and marketing for Orval Kent Food Company, the country's largest manufacturer of prepared salads.

His accomplishments in these unrelated industries provide some insight into his passion and leadership skills. He also brings the same passion to his speaking where he speaks to many corporate audiences on a variety of topics, including leadership, motivation, and team building.

Mac has authored or co-authored twenty-two books that have sold over four million copies. His titles include:

- *Change is Good ... You Go First*
- *Charging the Human Battery*
- *Customer Love*
- *Finding Joy*
- *Learning to Dance in the Rain*
- *Leadership Quotes*
- *212° Leadership*
- *212°: The Extra Degree*
- *212° Service*
- *Habits Die Hard*
- *Motivational Quotes*
- *One Choice*
- *The Nature of Success*
- *The Secret of Living is Giving*
- *The Power of Attitude*
- *The Power of Kindness*
- *The Essence of Leadership*
- *The Road to Happiness*
- *The Dash*
- *To a Child, Love is Spelled T-I-M-E*
- *You Can't Send a Duck to Eagle School*
- *What's the Big Idea?*

For more information about Mac, visit www.simpletruths.com

BJ Gallagher is an inspirational author, speaker, and storyteller. Her books, keynote speeches, and workshops are designed to educate, entertain, and enlighten people—consistently focusing on the "power of positive doing."

She has written over two dozen books, including an international best-seller, *A Peacock in the Land of Penguins*, now published in 23 languages worldwide. Her other Simple Truths books include:

- *Learning to Dance in the Rain: The Power of Gratitude*
- *The Best Way Out is Always Through: The Power of Perseverance*
- *Oh, Thank Goodness, It's Not Just Me!*
- *Oil for Your Lamp: Women Taking Care of Themselves*

BJ is a much-in-demand keynote speaker, making frequent presentations at conferences and professional gatherings in the United States, Asia, Europe and Latin America. Her lively presentations inspire and instruct audiences of all types—with a style that is up-beat, fast-paced, funny, dynamic, and charismatic.

Her impressive client list includes: IBM, Chrysler Corporation, Chevron, Southern California Edison, Los Angeles Times, Phoenix Newspapers Inc., American Press Institute, Atlanta Journal-Constitution, Raytheon, John Deere Credit, TRW, Farm Credit Services of America, U.S. Department of Interior, the American Lung Association, Marathon Realty (Canada), and many others.

To find out more about BJ, her books, and her speaking topics, visit her at: www.bjgallagher.com or www.womeneed2know.com

*It is not easy to find*

## *happiness*

*in ourselves, and it is not possible to find it elsewhere.*

*≈ Agnes Repplier, essayist and writer ≈*

*If you have enjoyed this book we invite you to check out
our entire collection of gift books, with free inspirational movies,
at www.simpletruths.com. You'll discover it's a great way to inspire friends
and family, or to thank your best customers and employees.*

143